WRESTLING SUPERST★RS

CHRIS JERICHO

BY RAY McCLELLAN

EPIC

BELLWETHER MEDIA • MINNEAPOLIS, MN

EPIC BOOKS are no ordinary books. They burst with intense action, high-speed heroics, and shadows of the unknown. Are you ready for an Epic adventure?

This edition first published in 2015 by Bellwether Media, Inc.

No part of this publication may be reproduced in whole or in part without written permission of the publisher. For information regarding permission, write to Bellwether Media, Inc., Attention: Permissions Department, 5357 Penn Avenue South, Minneapolis, MN 55419.

Library of Congress Cataloging-in-Publication Data

McClellan, Ray.
  Chris Jericho / by Ray McClellan.
    pages cm. – (Epic: Wrestling Superstars)
Includes bibliographical references and index.
  Summary: "Engaging images accompany information about Chris Jericho. The combination of high-interest subject matter and light text is intended for students in grades 2 through 7"– Provided by publisher.
  ISBN 978-1-62617-140-4 (hardcover : alk. paper)
  1. Jericho, Chris–Juvenile literature. 2. Wrestlers–Canada–Biography–Juvenile literature. I. Title.
  GV1196.J47M33 2014
  796.812092–dc23
  [B]

2014010778

Printed in the United States of America, North Mankato, MN.

TABLE OF CONTENTS

WARNING!

The wrestling moves used in this book are performed by professionals.
Do not attempt to reenact any of the moves performed in this book.

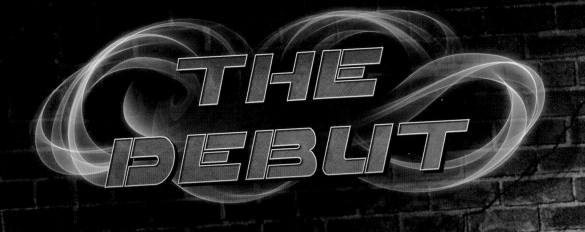

THE DEBUT

Chris Jericho meets Road Dogg in the ring. Jericho has a lot to prove. Two weeks earlier he introduced himself as a wrestling hero for a new era.

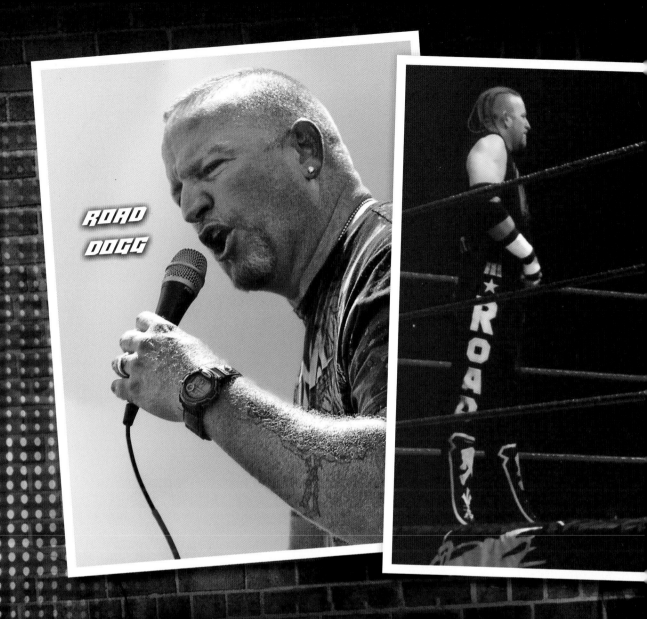

ROAD DOGG

Control of the match shifts back and forth. Eventually, Jericho powerbombs Road Dogg through a table. This disqualifies Jericho in his debut. Still, Y2J has made a mark on WWE.

WHO IS CHRIS JERICHO?

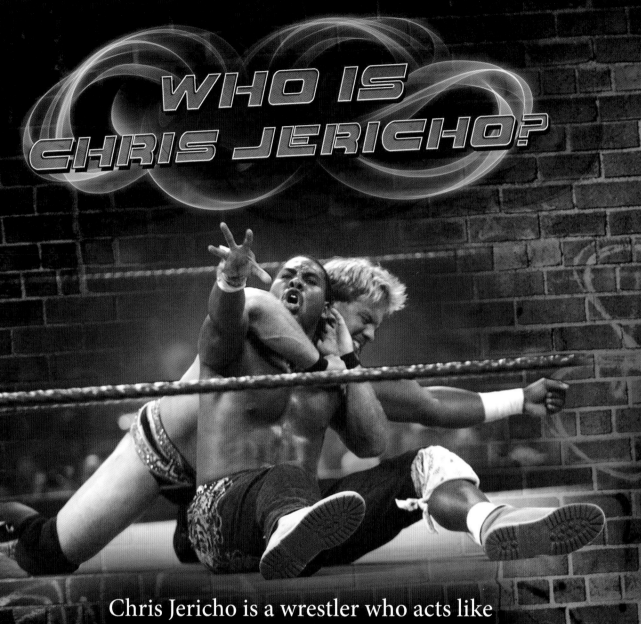

Chris Jericho is a wrestler who acts like a rock star. He is known as the Ayatollah of Rock 'n' Rolla. His championship wins put his name among the WWE greats.

REAL LIFE ROCK STAR

Jericho also sings in a heavy metal band called Fozzy.

LIFE BEFORE WWE

Jericho grew up around sports. His dad played hockey in the NHL. Their family watched wrestling events together. Jericho also fought friends for fun.

TED IRVINE

Jericho's father is named
Ted Irvine. He played for
four teams in the NHL.

At age 19, Jericho trained at the Hart Brothers Pro Wrestling Camp. Soon after, he wrestled in matches around Canada. Later he performed in Japan, Mexico, and Germany.

Jericho has written books about his life before and during his WWE career.

NEW YORK TIMES BESTSELLING AUTHOR

CHRIS JERICHO
WITH PETER THOMAS FORNATALE

UNDISPUTED

HOW TO BECOME THE WORLD CHAMPION IN 1,372 EASY STEPS

A WWE SUPERSTAR

STAR PROFILE

WRESTLING NAME:	Chris Jericho
REAL NAME:	Christopher Keith Irvine
BIRTHDATE:	November 9, 1970
HOMETOWN:	Winnipeg, Manitoba, Canada
HEIGHT:	6 feet (1.8 meters)
WEIGHT:	226 pounds (103 kilograms)
WWE DEBUT:	1999
FINISHING MOVE:	Codebreaker

Finally, Jericho landed at WWE. He soon became the first Undisputed Champion in the league. He held two important titles at the same time.

Jericho has collected many belts.
He became a Triple Crown Champion in
2001. He has also been the Intercontinental
Champion nine times. This is more than any
other wrestler.

WINNING MOVES

WALLS OF JERICHO

Few wrestlers escape the Walls of Jericho. This signature move is a hold. Jericho grabs an opponent's legs and flips him facedown. Then he sits on the wrestler's back.

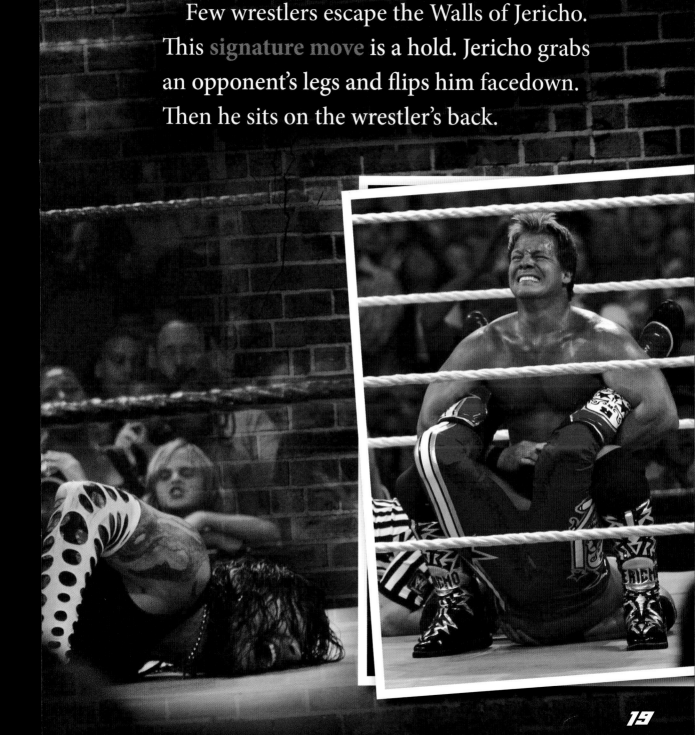

CODEBREAKER

Jericho's finishing move is the Codebreaker. It begins with a head grab. Then Jericho falls backward with his knees to the opponent's head. In your face!

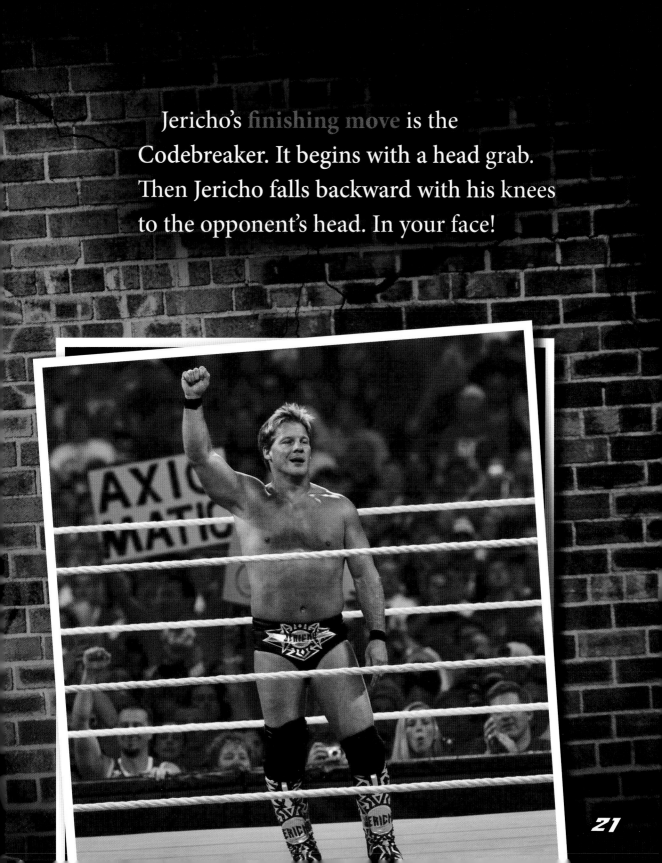

GLOSSARY

ayatollah—a high-ranking religious leader

debut—first official appearance

disqualifies—removes from a competition due to rule-breaking

era—a period of time that is set apart from others

finishing move—a wrestling move that finishes off an opponent

intercontinental—involving more than one continent

league—a group of people or teams united by a common activity

powerbombs—lifts an opponent into the air and then slams him down on his back

signature move—a move that a wrestler is famous for performing

titles—championships

Triple Crown Champion—a WWE wrestler who has won three different championships

undisputed—accepted without argument

TO LEARN MORE

At the Library

Black, Jake. *WWE General Manager's Handbook*. New York, N.Y.: Grosset & Dunlap, 2012.

Markegard, Blake. *John Cena*. Minneapolis, Minn.: Bellwether Media, 2015.

West, Tracey. *Race to the Rumble*. New York, N.Y.: Grosset & Dunlap, 2011.

On the Web

Learning more about Chris Jericho is as easy as 1, 2, 3.

1. Go to www.factsurfer.com.

2. Enter "Chris Jericho" into the search box.

3. Click the "Surf" button and you will see a list of related web sites.

With factsurfer.com, finding more information is just a click away.